KAREN CA

MIXED MEDIA
Magic

Art Techniques that Educate with Fun Projects that Inspire!

About this book

The madness and magic that can be created when working with so many phenomenal media available on the market today is so thrilling and so rewarding I just HAD to share my knowledge and love of this craziness with my students so they could get a little taste of the fun that I have each and every day!

On the outside I may come across as a fancy schmancy artist, teacher and author but when you boil it down, I'm no more than a straight up fun junkie. Oh, and also perhaps an art supply hoarder. Yeah, definitely that too. (And I know some of you are too! Don't deny it!) But unless you know how to begin or where to start with those supplies, your stash may be hindering your creativity instead of enabling it! As entering such a world can be a bit daunting, what with all the plethora of supplies one can choose, I have created this book so that creative souls of all abilities and backgrounds could have a basic understanding of mixed media supplies, principles and projects. After reading this book, anyone can get started on this amazing path, with confidence, as soon as possible! With every new art project success comes confidence, and with increased confidence comes relaxation, artistic freedom and sooooo much more FUN (and therein lies the magic)! So what are you waiting for? Let's do this!

Dedicated to my family. You guys are the best!

Author, Illustrator, Publisher: Karen Campbell
www.karencampbellartist.com
Book Layout and Digital Design: KT Design, LLC
www.ktdesignllc.com
Editor: Linda Duvel

Table of *Contents*

What is

What is mixed media? Well, first and foremost it is pure FUN! But if you have to define it, it is, quite simply, when a variety of media are used in a single piece of art. While this is a basic concept, the results and the possibilities are positively enormous!

For years, and long before I had ever heard the term "mixed media," I was a painter working with acrylics and was frequently commissioned to create simple paintings and murals. So many times, I would find myself in a tight corner, furrow my brow and whisper to myself, *Gah! If only I could use a pen to fill in this tiny spot right here!!* Or I'd find myself struggling because I was only using my gunked up bristles and inadequate tools. Those struggles, so I told myself, were just the trials and tribulations of being a true artist (insert dramatic sigh!). I truly felt I couldn't use a pen to color in a tight space because that would be cheating! What if someone caught me?! I honestly thought if I used any material or tool other than my paints and my brushes, my work would somehow become less than professional.

I lived (in fear) this way until I enrolled in my first mixed media art course. Afterwards, my entire concept of what was acceptable in art changed forever! I remember watching my teacher using paints and pens and sprays and different tools I'd never heard of before, on purpose, in the same project! I remember my brain slightly exploding and thinking, You mean this is a THING?! I can literally use whatever I want? Together?? Being able to mix and use any material on the same project, in order to achieve a certain result, gave me both artistic freedom and the confidence I truly never had before.

Having that level of freedom also gave me the power to flex my creative muscles in a way I had never tried before. Just having so many options at my fingertips inspires me to be creative each and every day! Did I mention it is fun?!

Having that level of freedom also gave me the power to flex my creative muscles in a way I had never tried before.

Most importantly, however, mixing materials gave me competence in areas where before I had had major shortcomings. Having permission to use marker and pens alongside my caked-up paint brush to have access to and perfect those details that used to get away, gave me a way to compensate for my weaknesses and even enhance and improve the whole finished project. Knowing how to dribble, splatter, spray and grab for anything and try everything I could get my hands on to create what I had intended, instead of simply always making due with what I had on hand, was also very powerful and exciting and fueled my creativity! More media options also meant simply having more resources on hand and for me, that resulted in better, well, results! Consequently, being able to mix and match materials in one project really enhanced my artistic skills and since has elevated my work to a level I hadn't thought possible.

Fast forward fifteen years and I can't even fathom the idea of being limited to one lonely art supply! The idea is positively ridiculous! Thanks to the growing popularity of YouTube, online classes and resources like this book, I hope that no matter where in the world you are, all of you will be able to be inspired, knowing you have the freedom to use as many artistic media as your heart desires (and your wallet allows!). I promise you, the results and the creativity one can gain from this approach can be powerful, fun and altogether magical. Don't believe me? Continue reading and you'll see!

Watch the making of at
bit.ly/mixedmediafun

Paint

But before we paint, there is (almost) always Gesso.

Gesso

What the heck is it and why is it used so frequently? Gesso, in its most basic form and application, is a primer made up of a binder, chalk, some chemicals that ensure longevity, and a pigment (either white, black or grey). Commercially made gallery-wrapped canvases that are white or black, are already coated with gesso and are ready to go! If you are starting with a surface not already treated, it is a great idea (and super easy) to coat it with gesso yourself. It is also great for preparing surfaces other than traditional canvases like wood, pages of a book, or watercolor paper. You just apply a thin layer over your substrate, wait for it to dry, and then begin!

White gesso has a lot of additional uses too! I use it as an alternative to white paint. It dries to a transparent, milky shade and I love to mix and blend it in with my skin colors

Gesso helps blend my skin colors to perfection!

9

when painting portraits. I also use it alone on top of and mixed in with acrylics as a cool, less aggressive, (opaque) white color.

Black gesso, on the other hand, is fervently opaque and is simply divine at completely covering up practically any and all layers of color and collage underneath it!

Grey gesso, in my experience, does not have the opaque qualities of the black, and works more like the white

in its coverage. Obviously, you can also just mix the black and white varieties to create your own desired shade, but pre-mixed grey is available in stores.

Awesome Acrylics

One would think that the world of acrylic paint would be pretty self-explanatory but, in fact, there's a whole big wide world out there and tons to choose from! Besides color and transparency, the best part about choosing one's paint (for me at least) is that these days, paint comes in many forms of viscosity! Right out of the tube you can choose if you want a thick and blobby paint (heavy body), a thin and creamy paint (soft body), a thin and runny paint (fluid), or one that is so thin you can use it in your fountain pen (high flow or ink)! How fun is that?

There are also a ton of mixing mediums you can purchase that change the nature of your paints as well. Depending on the product you choose, you can make your painting or project, chunky and lumpy, or gooey and stringy, runny or drippy, glassy or sandy, or make it also be able to stick to things! The possibilities are endless and totally fun!

Of all the gloss, satin and matte mix-ins on the market, I use Matte Medium the most frequently. Most of the time I actually use it for its adhesive properties and don't mix it in with my paints at all, but I could if I wanted to! Gel Mediums work just the same and some artists prefer those, as they have a creamier texture. Don't hesitate to play and experiment with different products; they are all designed to mix in with your acrylics and they are all equally fun. So go nuts!

Other Media

The list of my favorite supplies may not fit in this tiny allotted space; it is so long! There are also new products hitting the arts and crafts market every single day!!! So instead of listing off all of my favorites, I am going to organize this section into just two "types" of media, water-soluble and permanent, so that no matter what kind you are faced with or want to try out, you'll know if it's ok to use in your project (or not) based on its properties! Bottom line? There are no rules, so chuck as many things as you can into your projects and have a blast!!! On a lamer note, there are some guidelines and tips to keep in mind so that your masterpiece doesn't end up just a plain mess. I'm compiling a list right here to help you make good choices!

Water-soluble vs. Permanent

My Favorite Water-soluble Supplies
The first thing you need to be aware of when choosing and using art supplies is whether or not your medium is water-soluble. What does that mean? It means the product will move or liquefy (or "activate" as I like to say) when liquid is added to it. Sounds weird right?! How about FANTASTIC!!!

Here are some examples of various water-soluble markers, pencils and crayons when used dry or activated with water. These supplies are surprising, unpredictable, and FUN!

Beware! Some media stay water-soluble after activation, while others become permanent! So be sure to read your labels!

I almost always use these water-reactive supplies in my very first layers because that's when I am freer to explore and play. If I don't like something, I still have time to paint over it. Another cool trick to keep in mind is that you can also use other liquid items to activate your products! Clear or white gesso, Mod Podge (my favorite), a baby wipe, or just your finger and its natural oils will all turn those marks into magic!

Also, you'd be surprised by how much has changed in the way of art supplies since we were kids! Did you know that watercolors, probably the most well known water-soluble supply, come in the form of pencils, markers, crayons and fun little lipstick-like tubes?! The choices are remarkable!

These are some of my favorite choices and brands:

- Stabilo All pencils
- Watercolour, Graphitone and Aquatone pencils by Derwent
- Inktense pencils by Derwent (which are permanent after becoming wet)
- Watercolor markers by Tombow, Winsor-Newton and Letraset
- Watercolor crayons by Caran d'Arche (called NeoColor II)
- Gelatos (those Chapstick looking things!) by Faber-Castelle
- Distress Crayons by Ranger

Using any of these products by themselves or together (with or without water) can create brilliant backgrounds, watercolor effects, smudge effects and more! And this is just the tip of the art supply iceberg!! There are many other brands and types available online from around the world; you'd be amazed at your choices!

My Favorite Permanent Supplies
Now let's talk about art supplies that are permanent! These are fantabulous in their own right for their dependability,

there are quite a few water-soluble products that are LOADS of fun but are dye based and not lightfast, (meaning they will fade). Again! Read your labels!

lightfastness and steadfastness in the face of paints, gels, water, light and time and whatever else you throw at them because they simply won't budge or fade! In this day and age, you will find yourself confronted with a plethora of options! Besides the acrylic paint I use in my projects, some of my favorite permanent art supplies are:

- China Markers (which are wax based pencils)
- Posca paint pens (which come in varying nib sizes).
- Pitt Artist pens by Faber-Castelle
- Colored pencils
- Micron Pens
- Archival Ink in any form (from stamp pad to dropper bottle to fountain pen)

Supplies I adore but skip in my Mixed Media Projects
Suffice it to say there are scads of products that I love and own and use by themselves, but do not often incorporate into my mixed media madness. This is generally due to application method, cost, durability, lightfastness (or not), their oil-based properties, or other personal preferences and include:

- Copics or other alcohol-based markers
- Oil based paints/products
- Chalk or oil pastels
- Dye based products

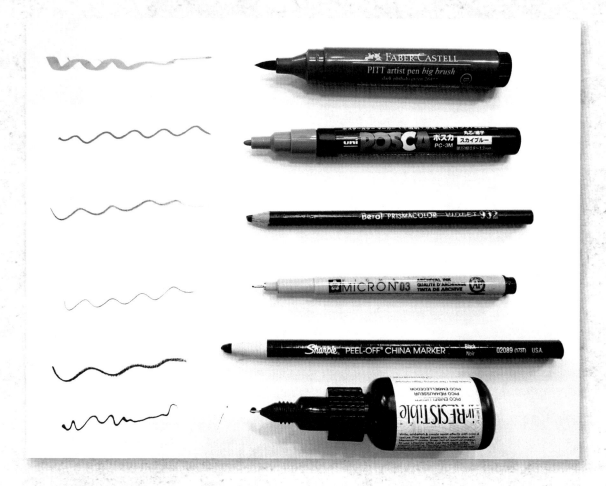

You, however, are making your own mixed media magic at home, so if it pleases you to use these items, by all means, do it!

The fun and MAGIC of mixed media is the pure level of excitement when playing and using these materials… and getting unexpected, dramatic, and playful unintended results! It's like a party on your paper!

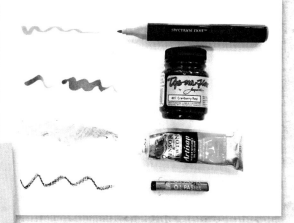

these types of products don't play as well with others and/or fade over time!

Tools of the Trade

How to tell if you're doing it right. Are you having fun yet? Well good! 'Cause that's really the only test that counts!

Have an old gift card lying around? An old utensil or comb? A putty knife from the garage wander into your midst? Some bubble wrap from a recent package? A broken pencil? In the world of mixed media, all of these items are fair game to paint with, make marks with, play with and make magic with! The sky's the limit! Oh yeah, and that old paint brush will work just fine too. Get out your paints and try smearing them around, starting with just your fingers, and then try to see what happens when you make marks using any or all of the aforementioned items. Having fun now?? I thought so! THAT is how you know you're doing it right.

Stencils

Arts and craft stores must have caught wind about the popularity of stencils a long time ago because their prices can be…yikes! Try going online to see if prices are cheaper. Better yet, hit up thrift stores and garage sales or make your own!

Another popular item to use with stencils (other than the traditional method of sponging or brushing paint through its holes) is to use a palette or putty knife to swipe Modeling Paste through them. Once dried, it leaves behind crazy-cool textures and ridges in the shape of the stencil that you can then paint and draw over!

You can also make your own stencils designs by using your glue gun! Squiggle out a design, let dry and go!

Stamps

Store-bought stamps are another popular item to use in mixed media projects! You can buy them or make them easily if you're creative. Brush paint or ink directly on a section of bubble wrap to make stylish polka dots on your piece! Carve out a shape from Styrofoam, a large eraser, or even a fresh potato to create custom stamps! Found items with distinctive shapes like toilet paper rolls, rocks and sea shells also make magic when mixed with a little ink and allowed to stomp across your creations! The sky is the limit, so get creative and get going!!!

Ephemera & findings

If you're ever in doubt about your project, please remember there is only one rule: there ARE NO rules! If you want to use an item for your art project, consider giving yourself a permanent green light and just go add it! Also popular are craft papers, tissue papers, napkins, vintage papers, findings, letters, calendars, book pages, buttons, sequins, ribbons, fabric, do-dads, fake jewels, glitter, trinkets, ledgers, dictionary pages; the list goes on! If you can embed it or glue it, fling it, affix it, clip it or rip it, chances are, you can use!!

Watch the making
of this project here!
bit.ly/redhairfairy

Substrates

What are you going to "art" upon?

Canvas and Canvas Boards

Mixed media work is messy and fun! Consider starting with an traditional canvas. If you find your work becomes too heavy because of the media, ephemera and findings, then consider a canvas board. It is a much more affordable alternative to traditional canvas with a flat, solid interior structure that is sturdy enough to support whatever you try to attach to it! Cradle boards are essentially store-bought wood canvases and are gorgeous (but pricier) alternatives to canvas as well.

Wood scraps and wood cuts are great too!

Paper Matters

There are loads of artsy papers on the market. If I had to narrow it down to only one choice out of a million though, I'd choose a heavy 140 lb. Watercolor Paper each and every time. It is just as durable as canvas and stands up to collage, glue, layers and layers of paint. End of story. The only things you may want to keep in mind in choosing your watercolor paper is price (it varies greatly) and textures (which also vary greatly).

Hot press is smooth, while Cold Press is rougher, and Rough Press is rougher still!

Art Journals

There is an entire global movement dedicated to art journaling and it is one of my FAVORITE pastimes. In a nutshell, you create works within in the pages of a book, rather than on individual canvases or sheets of paper. The journal could be a blank store-bought book, a hand bound book, or an upcycled book found at a thrift store! My favorite type of book is of the found variety. The process of using a found book is known as "altering" a book. I like to find old art books that are rather large in size with nice matte pages. I have created many of these and they are my prized possessions!

Use masking tape to repair rips and tears and to reinforce old seams. It accepts paint and gesso very well!

You can also make your own art journals. I even once made one out of cereal boxes!! My oldest son and I ate the same cereal, day after day, until we accrued a giant stack of the same size cardboard rectangles. I then taped each page together with wide masking tape and the spine with decorative duct tape until my "book" was complete. Each and every page was then covered in white gesso and then painted until every last page became a masterpiece!
Check it out on the next page.

Single Sheets

As previously mentioned, painting or working on any type of paper is possible thanks to our friend, gesso. I've painted over single sheets of telephone books, vintage cook books, children's coloring books, you name it!

Foam heads, altered paint brushes, wine glasses, shoes

You may be sensing a theme by now…if you can stick stuff to it or paint on it, it's fair game for a mixed media project! Now let's get started already!!!

Watch the making of my cereal box journal here!
bit.ly/cerealboxjournal

Wanna take
a peek at the
completed
projects inside?
Go here!

bit.ly/finishedartjournal

Make instant backgrounds!
Keep a journal or extra
canvases out at all times...
instead of rushing to wash
dirty brushes during a project,
wipe off the excess paint
onto blank pages in your
journal/canvas! Then next
time you feel inspired to
paint, you'll have a head start!

Backgrounds

Backgrounds play a major role in your mixed media masterpiece in lots of different ways! Backgrounds set off the (more) important foreground, create your color scheme, set the mood and fill in those boring blank spots. As making backgrounds can prove stressful for some people, I am creating this little list to help you steer clear of confusion and head straight for artful fun and success!

Tip 1:

Backgrounds go first. There is nothing more stressful than making a perfect subject and then trying to figure out how to weasel a cool background in and around it. So do yourself a favor and just do the background first. Since whatever you put down is not supposed to be the center of attention anyway, you can relax and just have fun at this stage! Which brings me straight to my second rule.

Is your brain and OCD personality holding you back from making the fabulous and whimsical pieces you love so much? Just think: think less, paint more! Give yourself permission to play!

Tip 2:

Making backgrounds should be relaxing, playful and fun…or you're not doing it right! The blessing is that nothing matters yet. This is your grand and one and only chance to truly play, experiment, try new products, let loose, make crazy marks, and get lost in the moment! Put on loud music and paint with your hands! Go outside and spray paint! The more loose and relaxed your background is, the more focused and awesome your subject will look on top! Layer and layer until you feel good. When you are in LOVE with what you've made, are energized by what you've just gone through and feel fabulous about moving forward, you'll know you've killed it! Still not happy? Wait for your layers to dry and start all over again. The dried collage, paint and mediums will dry and only add texture underneath that will then add to the interest of whatever or whoever shows up on top! Here are some tips to get you started:

- Paint with your hands!
- Use different spray paints!
- Use Matte Medium to glue papers all over the place!
- Paint a solid color everywhere and let dry. Stamp all over and make a complete mess and then take a brayer and roll white gesso over all of it.
- Use inks to dribble from one side of the canvas to the other!
- Put Washi Tape all over in different colors and then paint stripes of paint colors that match!
- Close your eyes and paint!
- Paint it all one color! Who says the background has to be complicated?

Tip 3:

Background should determine the color scheme of your piece. While you should be having an absolute blast creating your crazy (or not so crazy) background and playing, you should be thinking about your color scheme at the same time. One fantastic and easy way to create a successful piece of artwork is to make sure it is cohesive and that your foreground ties in with your background. The best way to achieve this is by simply repeating the same colors in both. If you have a yellow and pink background, you should have yellow and pink in your main subject as well. Think of your painting as an outfit; you need both pieces to match!

Tip 4:

The background sets the tone of the piece. Chances are, if you have a fantastically fun play session making your background, you've already set the stage for the piece as a whole. Let the flavor of the background inform the piece as a whole. If you create a lovely, dreamy, pastel page, wouldn't a lovely dreamy pastel person work best on top? Yes it would!

Here is one of my favorite ways to paint a mixed media background:

Reinforce seams and rips in old books with masking tape.

Brush or brayer on white Gesso. Doing so allows some of the images underneath to show through (which I like!). If you want to cover them up, use two or more coats. Let dry.

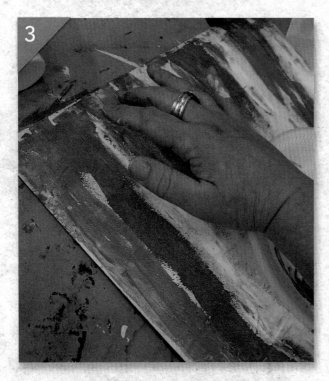

Take dabs of your favorite paint colors and use your fingers or paint brush (or an old credit card!) to apply the paint.

Add additional colors with washi tape!

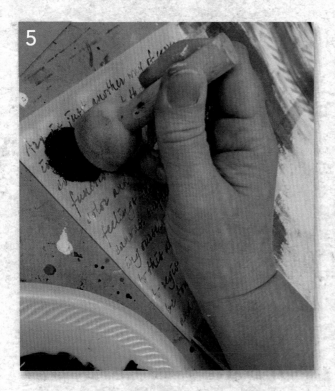

Use a stencil at the corners and randomly throughout.

Get out your stamps and add a few around!

Inspired by artist Jenny Manno

Rock your painting on top!

Ready to begin your own projects?
Let's go! ⟶

embrace the

glorious

mess

that

you

are

What a
Glorious Mess

I want to start off with an easy project to show you that mixed media doesn't have to be crazy, involved, or take up a lot of time to be successful, cute or totally cool! I originally designed this project for the fantabulous online classroom, *Mixed Up*, because I wanted to come up with a project that I knew even the most newbie beginners could master on their very first try! I love this project because there are very few supplies and no painting or drawing skills required so it is a guaranteed success for everyone.

Choose a quote that inspires you. Just remember, longer quotes may require you to have multiple words on each square. Begin with 6, 4" x 4" stretched and primed canvases. You could also use wood!

Special thanks to Katy Leitch for permission to republish this project!

Materials

- 6, 4" x 4" canvases (or wood blocks)
- 6 pages of scrapbooking or craft paper cut into 4" x 4" squares
- Matte Medium or Gel Medium
- Tim Holtz Distress Ink Stains
- foam brush
- White gesso
- Permanent archival ink pad
- Alphabet Stamps or Sharpie for writing letters

Choose 6 pages of scrapbooking or craft paper that appeal to you and cut them to fit each square. I like to choose all of my papers from the same book so that they coordinate easily.

Use Matte Medium or Gel to adhere your paper square to the surface. Make sure to coat both under and on top of the paper and use your finger to remove bubbles and wrinkles which may appear.

Arrange your grouping of canvases in an order that pleases you. To create balance, make sure you alternate lighter and darker patterns/paper.

Choose Tim Holtz Distress Ink Stains which best match your papers or use one to unify them. Vintage Photo is my favorite and adds that "antiqued" look to most everything!

Just because it's easy, doesn't mean it's any less fun!!!

Apply the stain all around the edges to create a "frame" effect. Blend with fingers.

Next, using a foam brush, use a scant amount of white gesso over each tile in towards the center or where your letters will go. This will help them stand out so they don't get lost in the color or patterns of your paper.

Using permanent archival ink and stamp your quote across the canvases. I like to vary my alphabet fonts to add interest and a touch of quirkiness! It is okay if they are not perfect.

Pass the ink pad itself, ink side down, along all the edges of the canvases or wood to accentuate the frame effect and add interest and edginess to your piece.

Use the ink pad to stamp additional designs around the lettering. Now you're read to hang and enjoy!

Fun (No Draw) *Flowers*

Isn't it refreshing to know that you don't need to have ANY drawing skills whatsoever in order to create magical works of art?! That's what this project is all about and I can't wait to see your versions of it!

Materials

things always look better in 3's!

To get started all you need are a few things:

- 11" x 14" Canvas Board/Panel
- Scrapbooking Paper (I like to choose a bunch of coordinating papers from the same pad)
- Sheet Music (Check your local thrift store!)
- Acrylic Paints that match your papers (I am using Burnt Sienna, Copper and Burnt Umber from Lukas)
- Matte Medium
- White Gesso
- Foam Brushes
- Stabilo All Pencil in Black
- Glue Gun
- Scissors
- Buttons

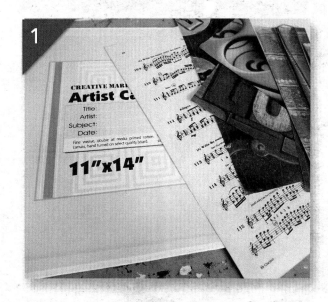

Gather up your 11" x 14" canvas board, sheet music and coordinating scrapbooking paper. Be creative! If you want to try this with bright and bold colors, go for it!

Now pick out 2 or 3 paint colors that match your papers.

Tear off 4 corners of one of the scrapbook papers.

Adhere the paper to the canvas panel using Matte Medium. Make sure to use plenty and apply it both under and on top of the paper.

Carefully glue down your sheet music in the center of the board. Again, be sure to use LOTS of glue both under and over!

Use your fingers to push down any wrinkles that have formed.

Once you have dried the glue, paint around the edges. Try to blend the paint colors into the papers so there is no obvious transition between paint and paper.

LIGHTLY spread white Gesso over the top of the sheet music. Make sure to spread some onto the frame portion as well.

Using scissors, cut out flowers. No need to be too careful, the wonkier the better! Each flower is made up of 3 different sheets of paper.

Try a unique design like a swirl if you want! Make sure the papers are different enough so that your eye can see all 3 papers.

Place your final paper cuts down on the sheet music and adhere using Matte Medium.

Using your Stabilo All pencil, draw stems and circle each circle flower cut-out.

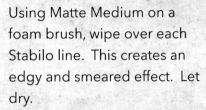

Using Matte Medium on a foam brush, wipe over each Stabilo line. This creates an edgy and smeared effect. Let dry.

Use a glue gun to adhere buttons in the center of each flower. Glue buttons on either side of the stems to represent leaves!

Stamp a cute pattern at the edges and corners.

Run your ink pad along the edges of your entire canvas panel to create a darkened "framed" appearance.

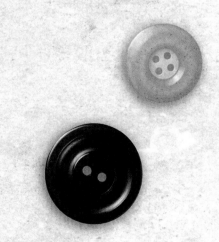

Glue Buttons on all the corners. Odd numbered clusters of 1, 3 or 5 look best!

Outline any petals you wish to further accentuate and voila! Masterpiece complete!

Using coordinating scrapbooking pages is a fool-proof way to pick a color scheme that works every time!

If you plan on completing the shading portion of this project, make sure you draw your face on watercolor or mixed media paper!!

How to Draw a *Face*

Since I draw and paint so many faces in my work both here and in my classes on YouTube, etc. I thought a little face lesson would be helpful and fun!

For years and years and years I was a creative, paint slinging soul who painted and drew loads of things for myself and clients. From Lighting McQueen to the Stanley Cup to a vase of flowers, I would paint it! I'll be the first to admit it though, during those times I prayed silently that no one would ever ask me to draw or paint a face because I was terrified and thought I could never learn how to do it!! Fast forward a few years and some simple lessons and whammo!! Faces are my absolute most favorite thing in the whole wide world to draw!

My hope is that after you follow these steps, you'll see how easy it is to draw too! Let's begin!

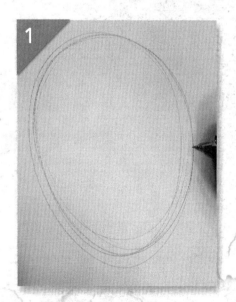

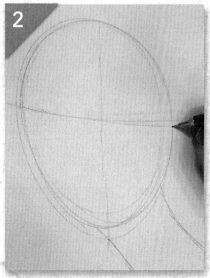

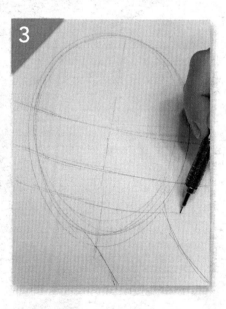

Draw an oval or an egg shape. Move your whole arm to make this shape, not just your wrist. Draw many if you have to and don't stop to erase, just ease into the motion!

With or without a ruler, draw a vertical line down the center and another across the middle. Add two lines for the neck.

Now draw a third line, halfway between the first horizontal line you drew, and the bottom of the oval. And a fourth line, halfway between the third line and bottom.

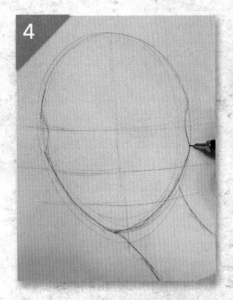

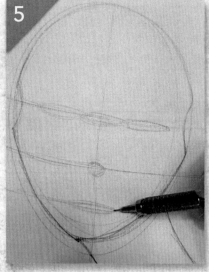

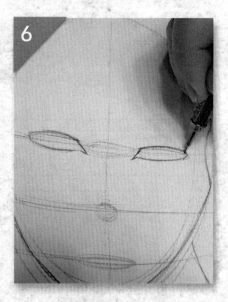

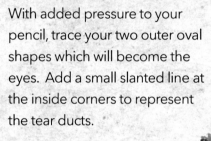

Draw slightly curved indents at the sides of the top horizontal line. Now darken the neck and face and jaw lines so you can see the outline of the face more clearly.

Across the top horizontal line, draw 3 squished ovals, all in a row, touching each other. And a small circle in the crosshairs of the middle line, and another squished oval on the crosshairs of the last intersection of lines. These are the place holders for the eyes, nose, and mouth.

With added pressure to your pencil, trace your two outer oval shapes which will become the eyes. Add a small slanted line at the inside corners to represent the tear ducts.

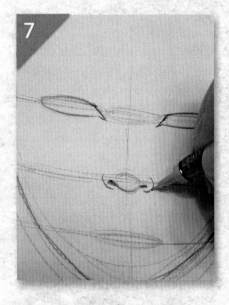

Outline the base of the small circle and darken little tiny ovals on either side to represent the nostrils. Then add 2 "parenthesis" on either side!

Now draw two slightly curved, parallel lines down from the nose. At the point where they end, slightly above the oval we had sketched in for the mouth, draw a "V" shape. Then draw two lines, flaring out from either side. Repeat this shape again and you've just drawn the top lip. Add a curved line for the bottom.

Erase any leftover, unwanted lines. For the hair, choose a point at the top of the oval for the part. Draw two lines on either side that go into the head oval shape, across the forehead.

Next draw two more lines that start at the part and go up and over the head oval. Hair has more volume that you'd think!

Draw two complete circles of the same size over each eye. Make sure that the top and bottom are crossing over the eye shape itself. Erase the top and bottom portion so only the remainder of the circles, inside the eye shape, remain.

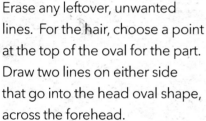

Experiment with varying eyelids by drawing a curved line over the eye. Do you want a dramatic lid or a smaller one? There's no right or wrong!

Next draw the eyebrows. They start over the tear duct and extend just past the far corners of the eye.

Add "c" shapes for the pupils. Your face is now complete!!!

Shading a *Face*

Now that we know how to draw faces (don't be like that, you really do!!), let's give shading a go! Follow this easy exercise to add some drama to your girls! All you need is three shades of watercolor crayon, pencil or marker a little water and away we go! I am using Tombow Duobrush markers in N75 (light), N65 (medium) and N15 (dark). You can use any colors you choose!

Using your lightest shade, add marks of color around the corners of the eyes, along the hairline, along one side of and under the nose (for drama!). Also color under the chin and mouth and hair, leaving some solid white areas on the hair as shown.

Now use your medium shade in the same areas, only use it more sparingly.

Go in with your darkest shade even more sparingly. Dip a watercolor brush into clean water and run it over your colored areas moving darkest to lightest.

Be careful where you move your brush as the marker will "activate" with the water and spread and flow dramatically!

Continue until all areas have been touched with the water. Be sure to leave some areas white. Let dry. Go back with your darkest shade in any places you want more shading or emphasis.

I chose to darken her eyebrows, some individual hair strands, and the corners of her eyelids and jawline.

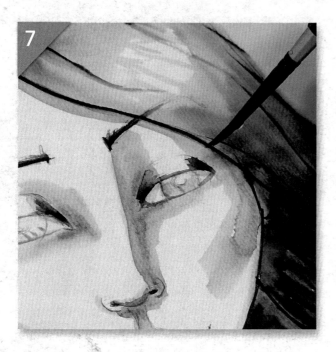

7

After paper has dried again, go back with a smaller brush and activate new areas. Let dry.

8

Using a fine tip Sharpie or permanent marker, define the irises, pupils and any other areas you'd like to see have more definition, like some hair strands!

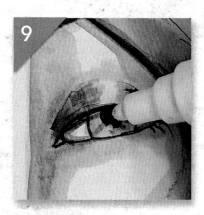

9

Using a white paint marker, add twinkles in the eyes, a touch on the lower lip and any highlighted areas that may have been lost due to over shading.

10

Admire your beautiful face!

HOT TIP!
Encaustic Wax must only be applied to a very strong and stiff surface like wood, metal or canvas board!

You can even skip the watercolor altogether!

Easy Encaustics

Did you know you can paint with wax? Crazy, right?! And people have been using it as their go-to medium for over 500 years! And while I know some of you are SUPER anxious about trying out Encaustics for the first time, I can assure you that it is safe, easy, fast and a BLAST! All you really need to get started is a heat gun, a crockpot and some Encaustic Medium which is available in fine art stores and online. You can collage, paint, embed, scrape and artfully layer with it, just like with other mediums. Think of it as Gel Medium…on steroids! But let's start off nice and slow and not get ahead of ourselves. No worries, this project is as delightful as it is simple!

This project was specifically designed to show you just how easy it can be!! All you need for supplies are the following:

- Small Crockpot (designated for art). I find that my local thrift store ALWAYS has these in stock.
- Wood piece of desired size. For this I am working small pieces that are 4" x 4", 4" x 6" and 4" x 8"
- Joint Compound or Venetian Plaster (available at your local home improvement store)
- Natural Bristled Brushes
- Laser Printed Images
- Encaustic Medium (1 lb. will do)
- Watercolors if desired (I am using Jimminy, Mermaid and Butteryfly from the Jane Davenport Brights set)
- Stamps and Ink Pad
- Ink for "splashing"
- Heat Gun or Hair Dryer
- Optional: White Encaustic Colored Paint and a separate, small, used crockpot for it.

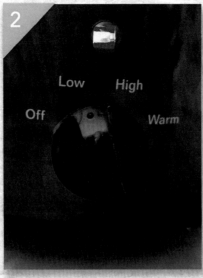

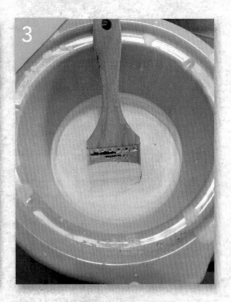

Pour ½ lb of Encaustic Medium into a small crockpot and turn heat to HIGH to get it to start melting.

Once a good portion of it has melted, turn heat to LOW.

Optional – Use a separate small crockpot for White Encaustic Wax (sold separately).

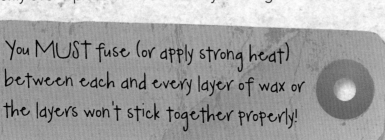

Using a putty knife, spread Venetian Plaster or Joint Compound evenly over a piece of wood. Let Dry Overnight.

Using watercolors with water, apply to the edges of your project. Use water to blend inward towards the center.

You MUST fuse (or apply strong heat) between each and every layer of wax or the layers won't stick together properly!

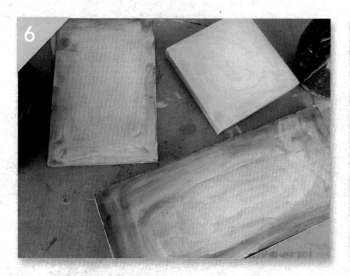

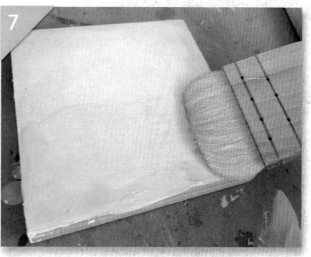

The darker areas around the edges will create a lovely framed look.

Once the hot wax has melted in your crockpot it is ready to use! Dip your brush into the encaustic medium and quickly apply a single even layer over the entire wood board.

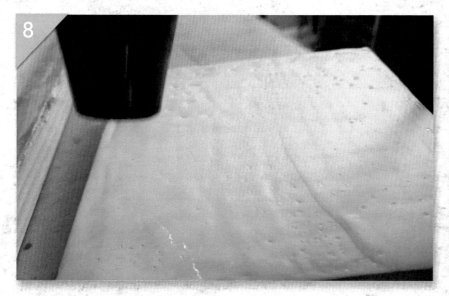

Using a heat gun (or hair dryer), heat the entire layer of wax you just applied. Starting at the top left corner, move your heat source slowly across the entire surface, letting each area become momentarily shiny before moving on. Repeat the wax and fuse, but this time go in the opposite direction.

While the wax is still warm, position the laser printed image face down on your substrate. Use a spoon and your thumb to push down and rub with strong, even movements until the wax has cooled (about 1 minute).

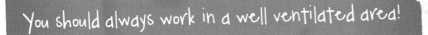

You should always work in a well ventilated area!

Using a small spray bottle of water, saturate the paper until you can see the image clearly.

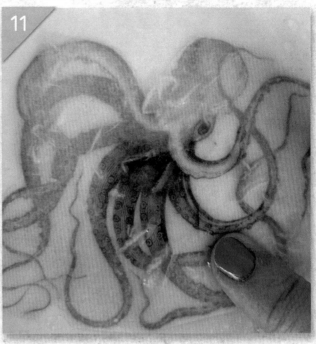

Lightly rub until the paper starts wearing away. Be careful not to rub too hard or the image will also come away. Take your time and be patient!

Once you have rubbed as much of the paper away as you safely can, run another thin layer of wax over the entire board.

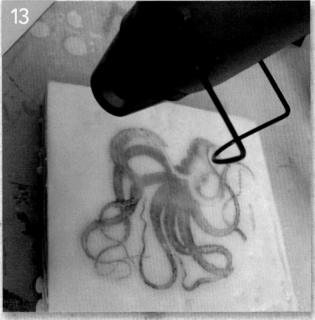

Now fuse. Again, starting at the top left and then slowly moving your heat gun until all the wax has been melted for just a second or two.

When the wax has cooled, decorate the edges with a favorite stamp!

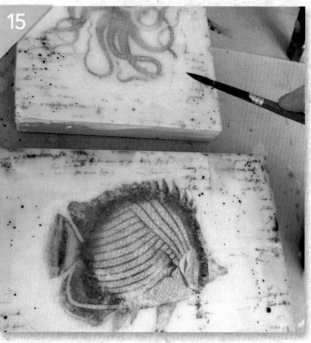

Using a long paint brush and permanent ink, splatter lightly around your images.

If you've chosen to also use white wax, you can use a small natural bristled brush to "paint" around the edges, as well as make fun splatters all around!

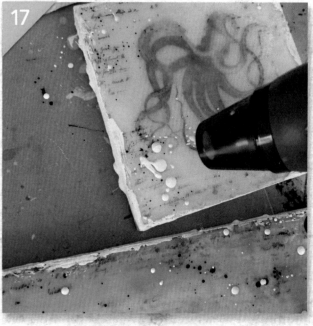

Don't forget to fuse! Those new fun splatters will not adhere to the layers underneath if you do not fuse them.

Dragonfly Girl
Background

Creating backgrounds with spray paints is super easy! It's fast, economical (each can is only $3-$8), super colorful and FUN! We will start out by using Matte Medium to adhere pieces of a colorful napkin to our canvases (mine measure 12" x 24" but use what you have/like!). I grabbed these napkins at a party store but you can pick up napkins everywhere from your local grocery store to the dollar store! Choose colorful spray paints that match the colors in your napkins for a fool proof color scheme! Then you can easily add black and white/silver for finishing touches. Think of your napkins as the shirt and your paints as your pants, they need to go together, right?!

These are three backgrounds I did all at once, because this girl has some pretty cute friends to hang out with! But obviously for the girl you'll only need one.

HOT TIP!

When doing a series of paintings, do all the backgrounds at one time so you they all go together!

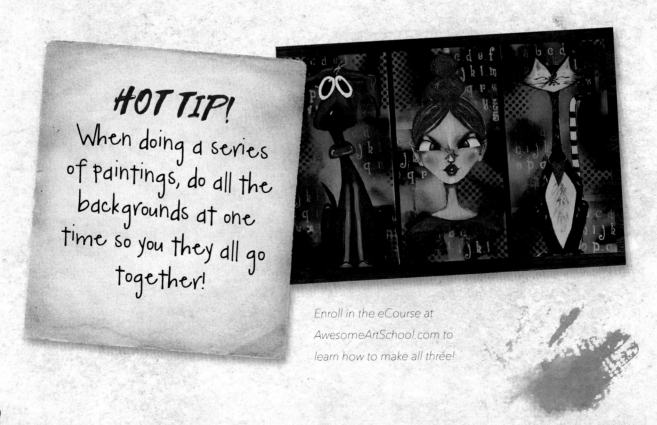

Enroll in the eCourse at AwesomeArtSchool.com to learn how to make all three!

Materials

The supplies I chose for this project are:

- 12" x 24" stretched canvases (3/4" thick)
- Matte Medium
- Sponge Brush
- Gloss Jungle Green by Krylon
- Fluorescent red by Krylon
- Satin Oasis Blue by Rust-oleum
- Satin Sumptuous Purple
- Black and Silver spray paints (any brand)
- Americana "Whimsical Delight" Alphabet Stencil by DecoArt
- Bubble wrap or dots stencils

I do tend to avoid glossy paints as they are harder to layer over than satin or matte. Let's do this!

Choose a pretty napkin (or tissue paper/ scrapbooking paper) and 3-4 colorful spray paints that coordinate nicely.

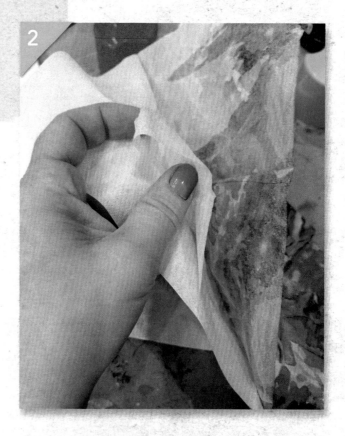

Separate the colorful napkin front from its back 1-2 layers. Peel them away so you are only using the top layer. Tear top piece into large sections.

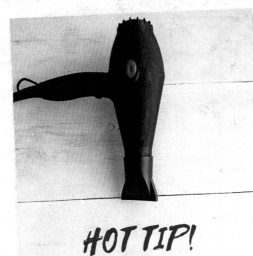

HOT TIP!
Use a hair dryer or heat gun to dry your projects in no time flat!

Use a foam brush to adhere the napkin pieces onto your canvas. Apply matte medium liberally both under and over the napkin pieces. Since spray paint has a large spray radius, you may leave lots of canvas white as the paint will quickly fill in these areas.

Outside or in a well ventilated/protected area, spray small sections with each of your 4 colors roughly 8"-12" inches from your canvases.

Make sure to equally distribute the colors around each one. Shake the cans often while spraying so the nozzle doesn't clog.

When you have a good distribution of colors, you many try your hand at spray painting through some stencils! I love how white and silver look through my alphabet stencil!

Use painted bubble wrap or a more generic pattern at the corners of each canvas. This will help create the illusion of a frame!

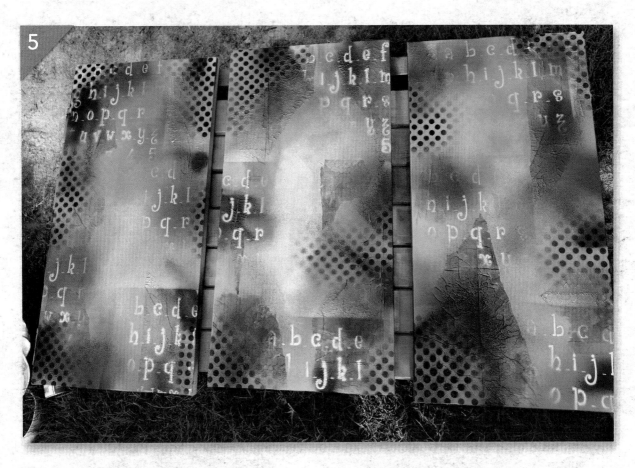

5

Stand back and inspect your work. Make sure they all look uniform. You can easily go back and repaint any areas that need extra touching up!

WATCH OUT!
Don't spray too closely to the canvas or you will get unattractive, large pooled areas that take a long time to dry and are hard to work over.

Dragonfly Girl

All set with your fancy schmancy new spray-painted background? Go grab it and let's get started on our cute girl! Now don't let this long list of supplies fool you, this project is actually super straightforward. All the complicated shading is actually just done with Gelatos and your finger. Zero fancy paint-blending skills required! Once you have a general sketch for a girl (or boy, or what-have-you!), you are ready to rock and roll! Use whatever paints you have lying around and whatever matches your cool background! As always, the list of supplies shown is simply what I used and in no way does it mean you have to use them too...
don't forget to have FUN!!!

HOT TIP!
If you're on a budget, just pick up 2 or 3 gelatos in skin tones plus white. You'll have everything you need to create glowing skin!

Materials

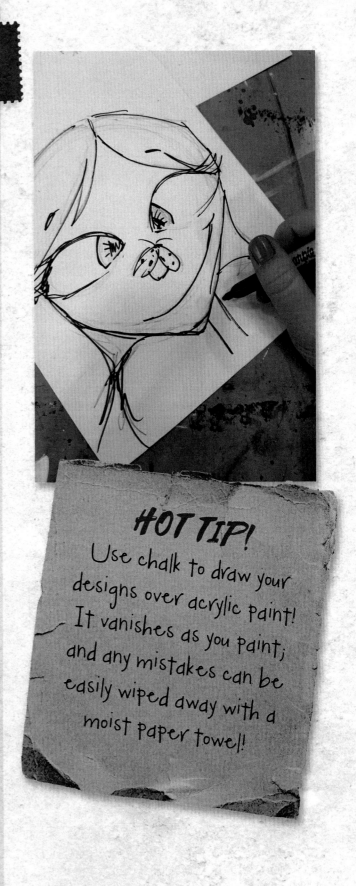

- White Gesso (highlights)
- Chalk (for drawing over background)
- Fleshtone – Ceramcoat (skin)
- Trail Tan – Ceramcoat (skin)
- Pink – Stabilo Woody Pencil (any watercolor or colored pencil is fine)
- Manganese Blue Hue – Liquitex Heavy Body (eyes)
- Fluorescent Pink – Liquitex Concentrated
- Peach – Gelatos by Faber-Castell
- Guava - Gelatos by Faber-Castell
- Metallic Melon - Gelatos by Faber-Castell
- White - Gelatos by Faber-Castell
- Rusty Hinge – Distress Crayon by Tim Holtz
- Black - PITT artist big brush pen (for outlines/lashes)
- White - PITT artist big brush pen (for highlights)
- Cold Grey III - PITT artist big brush pen (for shading white of eyes)
- Light Flesh - PITT artist big brush pen (for additional skin shading)
- Cinnamon - PITT artist big brush pen (for additional skin shading)
- Phthalo Blue - PITT artist big brush pen (to match blue of eyes)
- Pink Carmine - PITT artist big brush pen (red for hair & lips)
- White – Posca Pen
- Black – Posca Pen
- Matte Mod Podge (sealant)
- Americana Acrylic Spray Varnish (optional)

HOT TIP!
Use chalk to draw your designs over acrylic paint! It vanishes as you paint, and any mistakes can be easily wiped away with a moist paper towel!

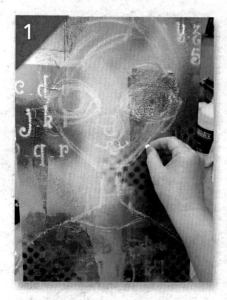

Using your design plan as a guide, draw out your character with chalk. Make as many changes as necessary until you are satisfied with her placement and your plan.

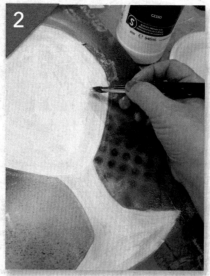

Apply 2 coats of white Gesso. A good thick coat now means easy skin work later!

Using a light watercolor pencil, redraw the features of the face and hair.

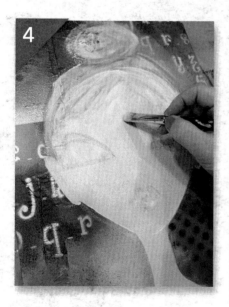

Apply one or two coats of a nice base skin color. I am using Ceramcoat Fleshtone.

Use a fun color to paint her hair! I'm super into fluorescents at the moment so here we go!

Paint the indication of a shirt in a matching color!

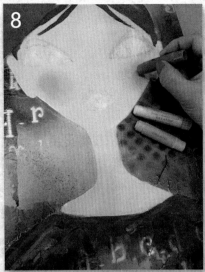

When the base skin tone is nice and dry, use a matching Gelatos color and rub in into the face and blend with your finger. Next, add small circles to the cheek areas in progressively deeper shades. Blend these out with your finger until desired shade is reached.

While the paint is still wet, blend in a little white Gesso.

Although Gelatos and Distress Crayons are both water-soluble, I rarely ever activate them with water!

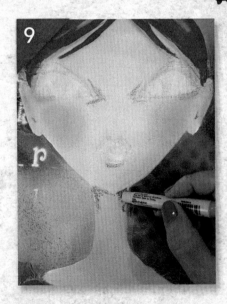

Next add a darker color (either Gelatos or Distressed Crayon) in the following areas: around the eyes, the ears, under the nose, mouth and chin. Blend these areas out with your finger.

Use white Gelatos or Distress Crayon to highlight the bridge of the nose, chin and forehead.

Apply darker paint to the corners of the eyelids. I'm using Trail Tan by Ceramcoat. Add Gesso to the middle of the eyelids for a lovely highlight!

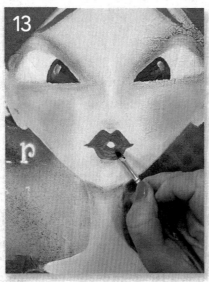

Paint the irises a pretty color! Add a highlight with white Gesso.

Paint the mouth. I am choosing the same color as the hair and shirt!

Add a fresh coat of Gesso to the whites of the eyes. This will make them pop.

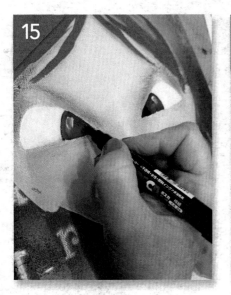

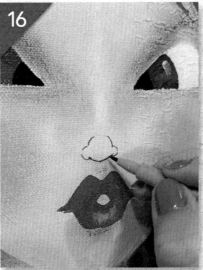

Use a black paint pen to draw in the pupils. I love Posca pens because they come in oodles of colors! Water-based Sharpies are a great way to paint in tight spaces.

Draw in the nose using flesh tone pencil or marker. I am using Pitt artist brush pen in Cinnamon. You can also use this color to outline the chin, neck and ears!

Slather Matte Mod Podge over your entire canvas. This step ensures that all the background collage elements and all the paint layers on top and all the yummy Gelatos blend and get sealed together.

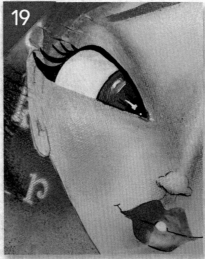

Use Pitt and Posca pens to add details to your piece! Pitt pens you can blend with your finger over the slick surface! Posca pens are filled with paint so those don't move the same way.

Use Pitt pens or a permanent fine liner in black to add details to the eyes, nose and mouth as shown.

Use a white Pitt or Posca pen to add highlights all over! My favorite highlighted areas are in the hair, eyes, on the cheeks, on the bridge of the nose, forehead, lips and chin. Oh! And the middle of the eyelids!

Use a punch to create a dragonfly. Ok but really let's get creative for this step! Use an image from a napkin! Dig out a picture from a magazine! There are lots of places we can go to find cute bug images.

Adhere the beautiful bug of your choice with Mod Podge and add shadows under the wings using a grey Pitt pen.

Add final shading (and drama!) to desired skin tone areas using Pitt pens in Fleshtone and Cinnamon. Add some final swipes of black in her hair and around her eyes and she is DONE!

Enroll in the Mixed Media Magic eCourse that accompanies this book! Only at **AwesomeArtSchool.com**

Want to learn to go from this...

...to this?

Fabulous
Foam Head

I know what you're thinking, "This project looks SOOOO COOL!!! But what the heck will I ever use it for?!" As a matter of fact, having a fabulous foam female in your midst offers up many creative uses!! Use it to store hats or wigs or sunglasses! Use it in your store as a prop piece or to show off merchandise! Give it to your daughter to hold headbands! Or to a sick friend to store wigs. What about a decorative centerpiece at a Halloween party or school dance? And don't ever tell me this wouldn't put a smile on your coworker's face when you station it on your desk wearing your favorite headphones. Any way you slice it, all of a sudden it becomes a must-have; *am I right?!* Luckily this project is SO fun, quick and easy (and a great one to do with the kiddos) you'll have a whole family of foam heads in your midst if you're not careful! Trust me, I should know!!

Materials

- One Styrofoam Head
- Foam Brushes
- Paint Brush
- Matte Mod Podge (or Glossy)
- Sparkle Mod Podge
- Tim Holtz Tissue Paper
- Lukas Cryl Studio Acrylic paint in Permanent Violet (or use your own colors)
- Lukas Cryl Studio Acrylic paint in Lavender
- White Posca Pen (I prefer to use the PC-3M size for my Posca Pens)
- Black Posca Pen
- Emerald Green Posca Pen
- Pink Posca Pen
- Pitt Artist Pen Big Brush in Magenta Bright

Start by tearing off palm size sections of your tissue paper.

73

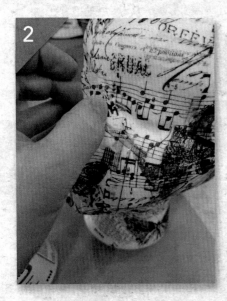

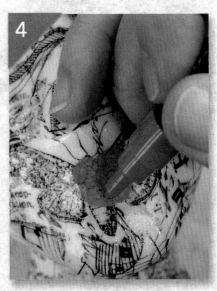

Using a foam brush, use Mod Podge both under and over your tissue paper as you glue it over the entire foam head, overlapping where necessary.

Once the head is completely covered with tissue paper and dried, apply a thin layer of Sparkle Mod Podge over the entire head using a clean foam brush.

Use your pink Posca Pen (or paint and a small paint brush) to paint in the lips. If you can't see the area well to paint, use your fingers to feel where the lips are.

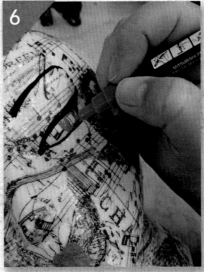

Use your black Posca Pen to outline the shape of the eye. Note the upper lid line passes through the eye area at a diagonal from lower corners up to the top corner. Extend the top line to create drama!

Still using the black, draw eyebrows about an 1.5" above the eye. Then draw the iris in the color of your choice. I am using my Posca Pen in Emerald Green.

Use a Posca Pen in white to fill in the whites of the eyes and your black to draw the pupils.

Make two dots on the pupils to bring your girl to life!

Apply a light layer of Magenta Bright with your Pitt Pen onto the cheeks. Blend in with your finger. Apply a second or third layer to make a more dramatic shade.

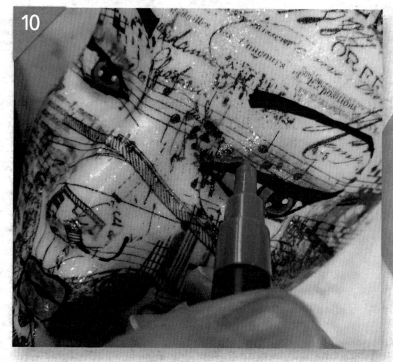

If you're hesitant to start the hair design, draw the outlines of the hair using chalk first. The lines easily wipe away as you paint!

Use Posca Pen in Emerald Green (or another desired paint color) to color in the area above the eyes to make the eye shadow.

Choose 2 shades of color for the hair. I am using Permanent Violet and Lavendar!

Start by choosing a part down the middle or off to one side. From this line, start applying paint down the sides.

In lieu of tissue paper you can also use napkins (make sure to remove underlayers), book papers, comics, or magazines!

Start with the darkest color first and apply a second layer with the lighter color or a mixture of the two to create a highlighted look.

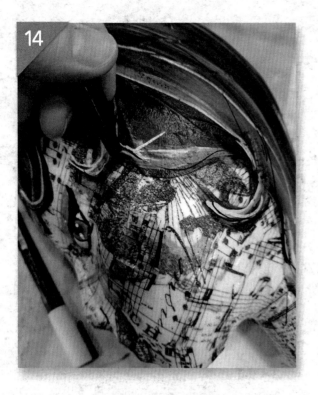

Use your white and black Posca Pens to add definition to certain strands.

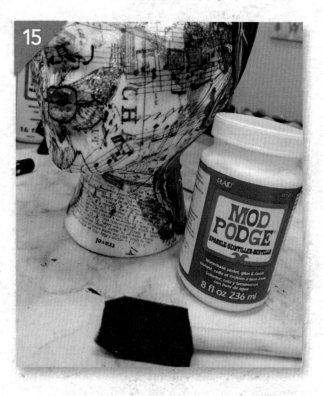

Finally, apply a final layer of Sparkle Mod Podge over the entire head.

And voila!!! She is ready to WOW!

Fierce Fairy Face

As much as I would love to take full credit for this project, I simply cannot without mentioning my good friend and artist, Susan Miller of Lighted Path® Coaching & Art Studios (Raleigh, North Carolina). It was through her Intuitive Soul Painting Workshop in April of 2018 that I learned some of the mixed media techniques shown to you in this project. Never before had I spray painted glittery goodness through a stencil out in the sunshine (oh my!! You must try!). Never before had I shot webbing out of a can and across my glorious jumbled hot mess of a colorful background! Never before had I poured over a poetry book looking for the perfect prose to match my mood. I hope the magic of that day shows through in this project, flows out of the pages of this book, and touches and inspires you wherever you may be on your own creative path. Such is the magic of mixed media.

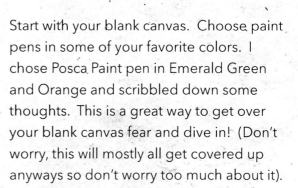

Start with your blank canvas. Choose paint pens in some of your favorite colors. I chose Posca Paint pen in Emerald Green and Orange and scribbled down some thoughts. This is a great way to get over your blank canvas fear and dive in! (Don't worry, this will mostly all get covered up anyways so don't worry too much about it).

As always, I will give you the exact materials I used on this project but please remember, use what you already have!! You can certainly use this list as a resource to help you make this exact project OR use the techniques as simply inspiration to take you someplace magical!

- 20" x 20" primed canvas
- Assortment of Acrylic Inks
  (I used the following by Daler Rowney)
  - Waterfall Green
  - Velvet Violet
  - Light Green (also used for eyes)
  - Rosa Fluorescent
  - Fluorescent Red
- Assortment of Large Stencils
- Assortment of Spray Paints (the more sparkly the better!). For this project I used Design Master in Flat White and Krylon Glitter paints in:
  - Candy Rose
  - Orange Burst
  - Sapphire Shimmer
- Tissue Paper (upcycled) by Brave Girls Club
- Bubble Wrap
- Assorted Acrylic Paints. I used Lukas Cryl Studio Acrylics in:
  - Fluorescent Signal Red (background and lips)
  - Fluorescent Magenta (background)
  - Apricot (skin color)
  - Golden Fluid Acrylic in Quinacridone Nichol Azo Gold (skin color)
  - Jerry's White Gesso (base color for skin and highlights on face)
- Posca Paint Pens in Emerald Green, Orange, Black and White
- Stabilo All pencil in Black
- Matte Medium (for gluing)
- Mod Podge (for sealing)

Use watered down acrylics or inks to drip your favorite colors all over! Make a mess and allow paint to spread all over until there is no white left. I used inks by Daler Rowney in shades of blue and green. I waited until my first layer of blues and greens was dry, and then dripped warm shades of pink and orange over it.

Grab some spray paints (the glittery ones are sooo fun!) and head outside with some large stencil designs. Spray and layer to your hearts content. I used white and a mix of Krylon Glitter paints.

Choose napkins, scrapbooking paper, tissue paper or perhaps papers from an old book. I chose to upcycle this previously used tissue paper.

Use Matte Medium with a foam brush to apply strips of paper amongst your spray-painted canvas. Then use inks in coordinating colors to blend the papers into the background design.

Make additional marks by applying paint to some bubble wrap and stamp around the edges to make a visual frame. I am using these happy fluorescent colors! You can also use more stencils or stamps if you like!

Helpful Hint

Cool colors (blues and green) and warm colors (reds, yellows) together make a mud color so take the time to dry your layers if you're unsure of how well they will play together!

7

Using a Stabilo All pencil in black, draw the head, ears, neck/shoulders of your fairy. With a paint brush, paint entire area with white gesso. I used a magazine reference to help inspire me. Or make up a girl from your imagination!

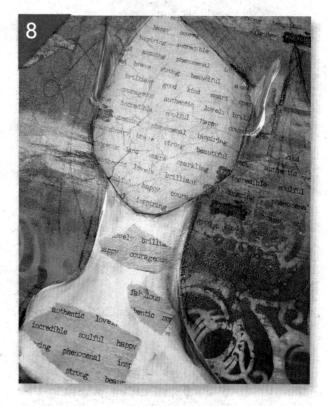

8

Take the same tissue paper that you used in the background and adhere it to the face and body with Matte Medium. You may skip this step if this seems too much.

9

Pick two shades of acrylic paint for the skin. Here I swept a very thin layer of Quinacridone Nichol Azo Gold around the hairline, eyes, ears and down the neck and shoulders and a bit of the lighter Apricot color by Lukas to blend the Gold into the tissue paper while leaving most of the tissue paper still exposed on her face. I drew the features of the face with my Stabilo pencil (see page 47 for how to draw a face) and painted her lips with my red paint pen.

Using the Stabilo All pencil, define the hair and draw strands from the head all the way off the canvas. Go over the same lines with a paint brush dipped in Matte Medium. This will spread the color beautifully! Use a white paint pen to color in the whites of the eyes and use paint or ink to color the irises. Use the same color to paint strands in her hair.

Use a stencil to create dangly earrings!

Remember, there are no rules; do whatever makes sense to you!

Use a bit of white acrylic paint or gesso to create subtle highlights on the neck, shoulder and face (on chin, tip of nose, forehead and on cheeks as desired).

Next you may wish to seal the entire canvas with Matte Mod Podge. This fuses all the previous layers together. Be careful when applying over the face as the Stabilo All pencil will activate with this action and you don't want to smudge her features!

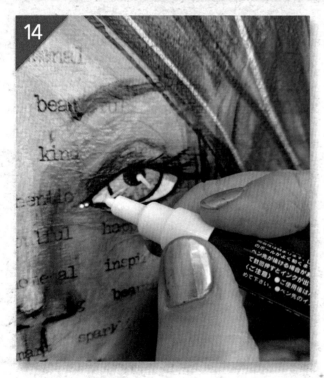

Use your white paint pen to add pops of highlights in her eyes, lips, earrings, hair and wherever you like a little drama! If you make a mistake, use a baby wipe to quickly clean it off.

I love to add streaks of white paint marker through the hair strands to give her even more drama!

If you don't have Mod Podge, you can also use Semi-gloss Gel Medium!

Use your paint pen to write out your most striking thoughts or inspiring quotes. I am writing lines from a favorite poem.

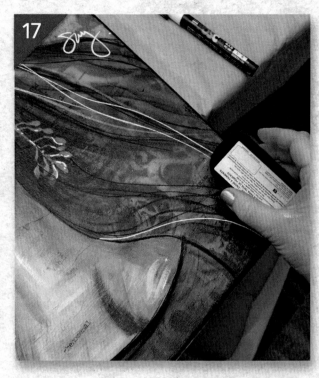

To create the look of a frame, run a black ink stamp pad around the edges of your entire canvas.

Helpful Hint
Paint the edges of your canvas black for a beautiful, clean finish.

For a super fun and edgy effect, I sprayed Webbing by Krylon all over my piece, careful to avoid her face. I'd never used this product before and man oh man is it fun!!! But again, this step (as all steps) are completely optional.

If you are too scared to attempt this on canvas do a trial run in your art journal first!

Don't ever be like them,
Darling!

Remember! You can always substitute!! Be creative and be brave!! If I use Tombow or other watercolor markers for her skin and you don't have them, just remember, any watersoluble item will do! You can use regular watercolors, NeoColor IIs, Stabilo Woodies, Gelatos, or even colored pencils that are not watersoluble at all! Don't have Pitt Pens? Use Posca Pens! Don't have any pens? Then just use paint! Just remember, this is art so (thankfully!) there are no real rules, only rules of thumb.

Be creative!

Don't be afraid to upcycle or thrift shop!

Choose your substrate and background image. I am working in a repurposed book and my background image is from a catalogue. Make sure your image is laser printed and/or matte.

Huge thanks to Kalman & Pabst Photo Group for Arhaus for allowing me to use their catalog for this spread!

Materials

I only list the EXACT materials because I know so many of you will want to know just to know (ya know?!) and others will want to know so they can experiment and play with new tools and others still will want to know so they'll know how to substitute with other supplies! It's all good! Whatever way you want to learn and play, enjoy yourself and give yourself permission to play around, make mistakes, try new things and just have fun!

- Laser Printed Photo or Matte Photo from Book or Catalogue.
- Elmer's Craft Bond Spray Adhesive (for gluing on background image onto page)
- Watercolor Paper or Art Journal or Canvas
- Watercolor Paper (inexpensive is fine)
- White Gesso by Liquitex (for general blending and use of white)
- Liquitex Basics Light Blue Violet (for sky)
- Golden Liquid Acrylic in Green Gold and Hooker's Green (for bushes/trees)
- Golden Liquid Acrylic in Pyrrole Orange (for dress)
- Golden Liquid Acrylic in Burnt Umber and Raw Sienna (for hair)
- Graphite pencil (I prefer GraphGear 500 .3 or .5 Mechanical pencil with 2B lead by Pentel)
- Matte Mod Podge (for sealing entire page)
- Scissors (for cutting out background and girl)
- Americana Acrylic Spray Sealer/Finisher (applied to girl before she is coated with Mod Podge so watersoluble supplies do not activate when she is sealed)
- Tombow Watercolor Marker in skin tones (such as 850 and 912)
- Aquamarker by Letraset in Mediterranean (eyes)
- Faber-Castelle Pitt Pen Big Brush Marker in Cinnamon, Light Flesh (for girl) and Scarlet Red (Shadow Accents on Dress) and Caput Mortuum (for phrase lettering)
- Posca Pen in Orange (for lettering of "Darling")
- Saral Graphite Transfer Paper (to transfer text onto page)
- Copic Multiliner 0.5 or Sharpie Fine point (to outline and for doodles)
- White Waterbased Sharpie Paint Marker (for highlights)
- Toilet Paper Roll (for stamping circles) or stencil

Tear out your background picture and glue it into your journal or onto your canvas. I used spray adhesive. Matte or gel medium will also work.

Choose acrylic paint colors that closely match your background picture.

Slowly add paint colors that blend into your background picture. Let dry.

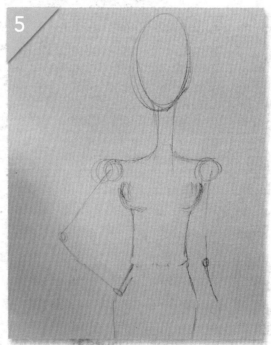

On separate sheet of watercolor paper draw your girl. Draw an oval for the head and a neck. Then rough in a basic form using sticks for arms and circles for joints.

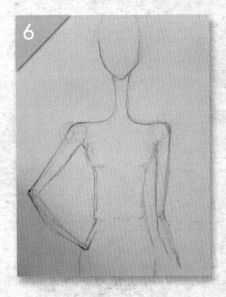

Once you have decent proportions, flesh out your figure.

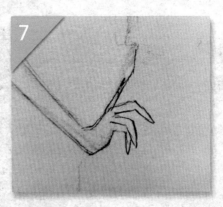

Do your very best to draw hands and fingers. Keep lines simple.

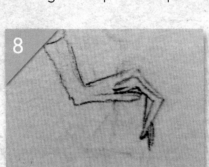

Now draw the other side. Look how wonky mine are! Just do your best!

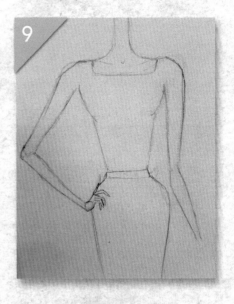

Add some lines to make a collar, belt and sleeves.

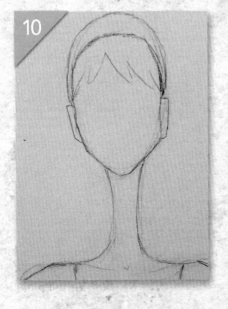

Starting at the top of your oval, draw the headband first. Draw bangs.

Draw 2 bumps for the hair and place the guidelines for the facial features. (Refer to page 47 if you need a refresher.)

Now draw in the features of the face.

Cut out the figure and adhere using matte medium or Mod Podge.

Paint your girl's clothes and headband. I am using a bold orange because I want to make sure she stands out from a crowd!

Now paint her hair. I do a single coat in brown and then a lighter coat on top for highlights.

Use Tombow markers in 850 and No. 912 to color and add shadow to all skin areas.

Add more drama to the face and clothes by using darker shades of the same colors over existing colors.

Using a waterbrush, run water over the entire face and shadow areas to blend the marker colors together.

Spray your entire figure with an acrylic spray/sealer.

Cover the entire project with matte Mod Podge. This ensures that the girl and background are properly adhered onto the substrate and that all the layers underneath are locked up tight!

After drying, use a fine tip maker to outline the features on the girl, as well as to doodle in and around your background!

Pitt Pens or Posca Pens in coordinating colors work well over the Mod Podge and can be used to add even more details, shading and highlights!

Perfect
Text

Print text from your home computer in your desired font and position it on your project. Helpful Hint: Use painter's tape to keep papers in place while you trace.

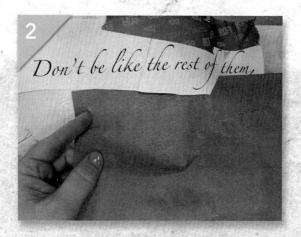

Place transfer paper, graphite face side down, underneath the paper. Using a pen, trace over your letter lines and remove the papers and tape when complete.

Now you are ready to color in the letters using markers or paint.

Stamp or stencil designs around the corners of your page for added interest and to help tie your color scheme together. Dip a toilet paper roll into paint and use it to stamp circles!

Don't be like the rest

Darling

Doodle with your pen to make extra lines and highlights on your girl's clothes and background images. You can also paint a faint line around her body to make her stand out!

Inspiration Station!

tips to a more creative life!

Watch the making of this spread while learning all about my best Mixed Media secrets!

bit.ly/mixedmediasecrets

Inspiration Station

Now that we've discussed supplies and techniques and done a few super fun projects, I want to leave you with some tried and true ways to help you always find inspiration when you need it most! These are my top personal tips to get you out of a rut, light a creative flame under your butt (sorry, I'm a sucker for a good rhyme) and get you actively creating RIGHT THIS MINUTE!

Have a bunch of Art Journals!

Keep a few art journals at the ready. I don't mean keep one measly sketchbook (although you should do that too!). What I mean is, make it as easy as possible to be creative by having art journals readily accessible, wherever you are. That way, when the inspiration strikes, you'll have no excuses for not getting busy! I keep a teeny tiny journal, fountain pen and waterbrush in my purse at all times! I also keep one in my car and one in my carry-on so that, no matter if I'm stuck in carpool or on a plane, I don't have to get stuck creatively!

Don't let $$ keep you from
Being Creative!

Leading an artful life doesn't have to mean breaking the bank (although it can and will, if you let it). Let's not kid ourselves, art supplies can be expensive. One way I significantly cut down on costs is by upcycling as much as possible. Instead of buying expensive blank canvases and art journals, do your masterpieces on cardboard out of your recycling bin (like my cereal box journal you saw on page 27), and in old books!

Bubble wrap makes the absolutely perfect stamp!

Don't forget you can make your own art supplies too! I made these cute hearts with a coffee cup sleeve!

I like to collect old records at my local thrift store (for only 50 cents each!). I melt the records to make fun bowls and then paint my mixed media projects on the jacket covers!

Bring your *Sense of Humor!*

While it is most certainly beneficial to art as a way to relieve stress and anger (everyone knows that art is awesome therapy), I find it helps my imagination and creative juices flow more freely when I am in a place of relaxation and happiness rather than anger and sadness. Having a light heart also helps put us in a mindset where we can forgive ourselves for our imperfections. A happy heart means less erasing, less frustration, more free-flowing ideas and more creativity!

While in Scotland, I bought this "eejit" apron (which means, essentially, "big dummy") and wear it when I art. It completely cracks me up every single time! Getting ready to get creative with a huge smile on my face is a fabulous way to start the day!

Fill your creative space with fun and cheerful things so that when you look around, your space brings a smile to your face!

Find work-arounds
for your weaker areas.

Don't let areas that you're not super strong in keep you from making amazing works of art!

- Not the best drawer? Trace!
- Having trouble putting thoughts into words? Look up quotes and see if you can find someone who has said it already!
- Need help with composition? Go on Pinterest and get inspired by new ideas!

A great example...my own handwriting is terrible! My work around? I always use stamps if I have something to say!

I decorated a corner of my studio space to help keep me in a musical mood!

Play music!
It's a catalyst for creative play!

Make sure you have music in your artful space. I like to experiment with different types of music and see how they affect my mood and creations! Try it sometime; it's fun! Blare classical music and see how that effects your brushstrokes. Try heavy metal and perhaps you'll opt for darker and more dramatic colors? Put on a throwback from your childhood or teen angst years and see what pops up on your canvas as a result. Who knows? Maybe you'll start dancing and your lines will too!

Clean Space = Clean Mind

I am a total slob. Ask my husband; he will tell you! But even the most naturally slobby people will get creatively stuck if their studio is so messy they can't even enter it. Trust me, I know!! So do yourself a favor and clean it up! Your mental cobwebs will also clear out so you can let the art session begin!

Challenge Yourself
with a limited selection of materials.

Often times when I find myself in a creative rut, I grab just one or two supplies (from my embarrassingly large stash) and pretend those are the only two products in the whole wide world I am allowed to use. You'd be amazed at what you can do with only a couple of things!

This project was done using only Graphitone pencils and water with a smidge of watercolor for the eyes. And DONE! Sometimes more is more and sometimes (when you're stuck) it's not!

In this project I challenged myself to make an entire journal spread without using a brush! OY!

Watch the ridiculousness for yourself!
bit.ly/funnynobrush

Go Online and find Artists...

Find artists that give daily/weekly/monthly creative prompts or follow challenges! For example, Jenny Manno is a California artist who posts weekly prompts in her Facebook group, Next JENeration Art. She posts an original drawing on Sunday mornings and your challenge is to make your own interpretation of her drawing by the end of the week! Here's one of mine. I've done many; they are so fun!

These two ways are always great ways to connect with other creative souls out there. So even if you live alone in Siberia, if you have access to WiFi, you can easily connect with other creative souls all around the world!

Here is Jenny's Prompt (done in pencil) and here is my interpretation (mixed media of course!)

Prep all your Backgrounds
in one sitting!

Ever feel the need to get creative but then have second thoughts as you turn to that daunting BLANK page in your journal? Well a great solution to this is to sit down and spend a day creating backgrounds! This sounds like a lot of work but if you keep your handy hair dryer plugged in next to you and dry the pages as you go, you can shoot through plenty of backgrounds in no time. Then when you are next feeling in the mood to create, simply open your art journal, pick your favorite background and get right down to business!! Make sure you vary the colors on each page and add some collage too! I like to use matte medium to glue napkins down on every 4th page or so, just to give myself more options. Since the napkins (or tissue paper) already have more than one color or picture on them, it just adds that much more to my piece! This is great for travel too; if you can only carry a limited number of supplies, essentially your pages will arrive half finished before you begin!

Have a Theme for Your Journals!

Have a watercolor journal dedicated to flowers, an altered book dedicated to faces and another yet for your urban sketches when you're out and about! This is a great way to organize your art supplies as well as your thoughts!

Find an Art Retreat!

Find an art retreat in your area, or (better yet) attend an art retreat destination in some schmancy area of the world! Nothing stokes my creative fires like an art retreat. There is something sacred and so purely enriching about creating amongst like-minded souls while learning new things. For me, that feeling of exuberance, inspiration and joy lasts well beyond the days actually spent at the retreat! Personally, I aim to attend at least one each year. It doesn't have to be in an exotic location either; sometimes just attending an in-person workshop locally has the very same, long lasting affect! Treat yourself. You're worth it and your art and soul will thank you for it!

In May of 2017 I traveled to Scotland to attend an art retreat hosted by artist Ivy Newport. Sketching on location and seeing new sites was so impactful. I am hosting my own retreat there with artists Lucy Brydon and Jenny Manno in 2019 and every year thereafter! Want to get a taste of what that's like? Watch and see in this fun video!
bit.ly/castleretreat!

We have reserved this magnificent 800 year old castle. Come join us!

Teach!

If you are one of those super creative souls (and if you bought this book, then I know you are!!) who is bursting at the seams to create, make and produce, and struggling to find like-minded others (or need an excuse to keep on keepin' on so your spouse doesn't kill you for spending all your money on art supplies) you should seriously consider teaching! You could teach privately at your home, host craft parties (I did this for years!), or see if your local craft stores or community education programs are hiring! Use your creativity to think outside the box. Teaching is super rewarding (both emotionally and financially) and it's FUN!

Still want more?

I got you covered! Sign up for my free online art classes at **AwesomeArtSchool.com**. You can also watch videos that educate and inspire 24 hours a day on YouTube! Visit me there today **youtube.com/karencampbellartist**

CHECK OUT MORE BOOKS BY
KAREN CAMPBELL

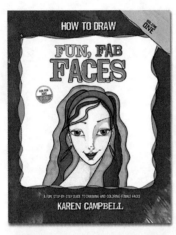

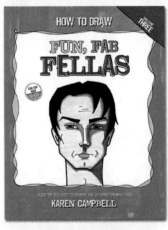

About the *Author*

Karen Campbell lives in the Raleigh, NC area and is a full-time artist. She is also the author of the "How to Draw Fun, Fab Faces" series and co-author of "For the Colorful Teacher," a hilarious coloring and activity book for teachers which she created with her co-conspirator Kris Miller (a creative sister-from-another-mister whom she loves and adores and appreciate more than words can express!). Karen also owns and teaches drawing, painting, and mixed media classes on-line at AwesomeArtSchool.com. She is most well known for her humor and straightforward teaching methods and for having waaaaay too much fun on camera. When she's not slinging paint, she's hanging with her ridiculously supportive hubs, three wicked cool kids and two adorable cattos!

While Karen has been art obsessed for as long as she can remember, it was her all-encompassing dive into mixed media a few years ago that really sparked an even deeper passion to create and teach. Thankfully, due to her propensity to always keep the camera rolling, you can take hours of real-time instruction from her through her plethora of popular (and insanely fun) online courses. Even more exciting is that you can witness over one hundred mixed media projects come to life on everything from oversized journal pages, to canvases to upcycled record jackets thanks to YouTube! Her mixed media work has been featured in multiple international magazines including *GreenCraft* and *Art Journaling* (both Stampington & Co.) as well as the fun U.K. based online classroom, *Mixed Up*, for which she has been selected to be a regular contributor.

Her next adventures will most likely be many more books that start with "F"!

Let's Get *Social!*

Check out my ***FREE*** art tutorials and paid classes!

- awesomeartschool.com

- karencampbellartist.com

- facebook.com/karencampbellartist

- instagram.com/karencampbellartist

- etsy.com/shop/karencampbellartist

- pinterest.com/karencampbellartist

- patreon.com/karencampbellartist

- youtube.com/karencampbellartist

Getting started on your Mixed Media journey and still confused about the process?

WATCH AND LEARN!

My hope is that this book shows you a lot of fun, varied projects to kick start your creativity! However, I realize it's easy to feel over-whelmed by the array of possibilities and the number of varied supplies out there. Indeed, there are so many! You may find it helpful to know that the bulk of my mixed media projects involve repeating the exact same processes over and over. I would like to invite you into my art studio for a quick tour and to teach you about my simple 7 step mixed media process! I think it will answer a lot of questions about supplies and how I get the lay-ered effect that I do. Just visit bit.ly/hamburgerseries and start learning today! It's free!

Made in United States
North Haven, CT
27 August 2024

56633394R00064